MW01611575

THE CRYSTAL RABBIT

6/17/95

Julie,

Anything's Possible!

Stephanie Mellen

**Story and illustrations by
STEPHANIE MELLEN**

THE
CRYSTAL RABBIT

Story and illustrations by
STEPHANIE MELLEN

Library of Congress Catalog Card Number: 93-91632

ISBN: 0-9637414-0-3

Manufactured in the United States of America

First Edition September 1993
10 9 8 7 6 5 4 3 2 1

DEDICATION

To my Mom - Aileen Donohue - without her
unconditional love, support, and words of wisdom I
would not be. . .

ACKNOWLEDGEMENT

To Mary Gazda and Crystal Fox-Kalil for being my inspiration of pure light, pure love and pure joy. . .

To Sharon Riedel whose sweetness, grace, beauty, and creativity are truly an inspiration for me to follow . .

Stephanie Mellen

*O*nce upon a time in a
far distant land, there
was a quaint toy
shop. The emerald
green-paned shop windows
were polished with love every day
by the gnarled hands of the bent, crippled,
balding Shop Keeper.

As the people walked by, men, women, children would quicken their step, each heart beating with anticipation . . .

What wonders would the Shop Keeper's window hold today? A ball? A hoop? A wagon? A doll? A clown? A music box? Cuddly soft stuffed toys of all shapes and sizes?

All who lived in the village and the surrounding countryside knew The Store was the place where dreams came true.

The most beautiful of all was yet to come, undreamt by any man, woman or child who was or would ever be.

Snow was softly
falling, icing the
emerald green
window panes. A
soft crunch, crunch could be
heard under each passing booted
foot.

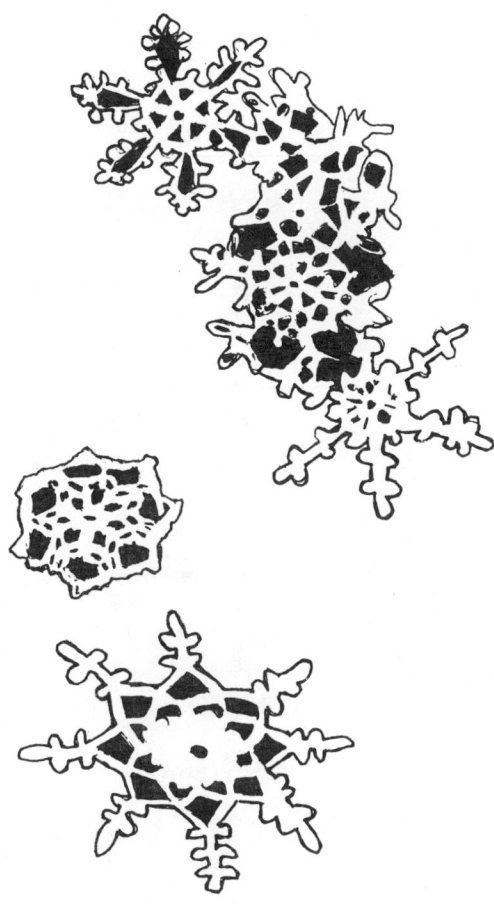

"Oooh! Ah! How beautiful! I've never seen anything so delicate, soooo exquisite!"

First two small children - a boy in a warm blue
coat with matching mittens and his older sister in a lilac
wool hooded cape - stood in amazement. Next a young
couple. Then the school teacher. The farmer and his
family. The baker and his helper. All with wide-eyed
faces pressing toward the snow-iced emerald paned
polished windows, gazing at the deep purple velvet pillow
with gold tassels on each corner.

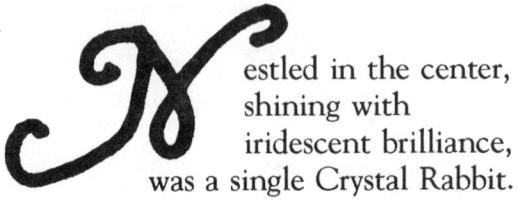estled in the center, shining with iridescent brilliance, was a single Crystal Rabbit.

The Shop Keeper's heart beamed with pride. *This* was *his* creation - made of the finest crystal in the land. There would be <u>no</u> price.

This toy was

NOT

FOR

SALE.

"Shop Keeper," the little boy in the blue coat with matching mittens asked hopefully, "how much is the Crystal Rabbit?"

"It's not for sale," the old Shop Keeper answered. "You may look. Don't touch or talk too loud - it might shatter the Crystal Rabbit."

"Ooooooh," whispered the little boy. He sadly reached for his sister's hand. As they left The Store, the little boy glanced, *just one more time*, at the shining, iridescent Crystal Rabbit.

Every day children,
parents, aunts,
uncles, the baker,
the farmer, the
school teacher would ask
The Shop Keeper if the Crystal
Rabbit was for sale.

Each time the proud Shop Keeper answered, "**No**."

Stephanie Mellen

*T*he shop window changed every week. A ball. A hoop. A wagon. A doll. A clown. A music box. Cuddly soft stuffed toys of all shapes and sizes could be seen through the emerald green-paned windows.

Each and every toy that appeared in the window was held, loved, purchased and wrapped with a great deal of care in lavender paper covered with tiny crystal hearts by the gnarled hands of the old Shop Keeper for *that* one special child.

Day after day, week after week, month after month, the iridescent Crystal Rabbit - nestled in the center of the deep purple velvet pillow with gold tassels on each corner - watched toy after toy being

held,

loved,

purchased, and

taken home to each special child.

Stephanie Mellen

I must be meant for
someone *verrry
special*," thought
the Crystal Rabbit,
struggling to hold back the
tears.

"*I have soooo much love to give! I
wish, **just once**, someone who loved me
would hold me and take me home with
them and love me*

F
  O
    R
      E
        V
      E
    R

and ever."

The Rabbit's tiny crystal heart quietly whispered,

"Anything,

anything,

ANYTHING'S POSSIBLE."

As the days turned into weeks and the weeks into months, the Crystal Rabbit's dream still had not come true.

Would the promise made by its tiny crystal heart *ever* come to pass?

ne cold, clear,
dark night,
after the
Shop Keeper
had wrapped the last
toy, turned off the lights,
put on his worn brown coat, hat,
scarf and gloves, and locked The Store's
bright blue door with a large, shiny brass key, the
Crystal Rabbit sadly thought,

"*What's wrong with me? Why won't anyone love me? Am I soooo terrible? Am I soooo awful that no one will ever hold me and love me?*"

"*Maybe there's a crack in my crystal foot. Maybe I'm just too different. I'm just not good enough!*"

"Anything's possible," quietly whispered the Rabbit's tiny crystal heart.

"Anything,

anything,

ANYTHING'S POSSIBLE."

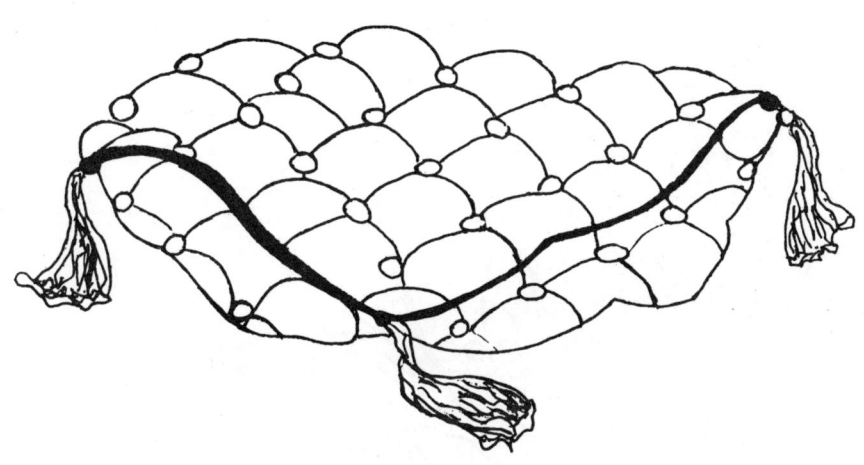

"*No it's not! My heart's breaking!*" and with that
the Crystal Rabbit shattered into a million iridescent
pieces, spilling all over the deep purple velvet pillow
with gold tassels on each corner.

s the sunlight
streamed
through The
Store's
windows, no toys
appeared. Not one ball.
Not one hoop. Not one wagon.
Not one doll. Not one clown. Not one
music box. Not one cuddly soft stuffed toy of any
shape or size.

"Oooh! Oh my! I've never seen anything so
delicate, soooo exquisite!" The whole village was
gathered, wide-eyed faces pressing toward the emerald
green polished shop windows, gazing at a deep purple
velvet pillow with gold tassels on each corner. Nestled
in the center, shining with iridescent brilliance was a
single tiny crystal heart.

A sign, hand painted in deep purple letters, hung at an angle on The Store's bright blue door,

CLOSED - - - FOREVER

"**NO!**" cried the little boy in the warm blue coat with the matching mittens. His sister, the young couple and their new baby, the school teacher, the farmer and his family, the baker and his helper, and the old Shop Keeper all stood with tears streaming down their cheeks as they looked in the window.

"If only I had let someone hold the Crystal Rabbit - *just once*," sighed the old Shop Keeper. "If only I had told the Crystal Rabbit how special it was. How much joy it brought me. Now, the Crystal Rabbit will **never** know."

Silently, on the other side of the shop window, the tiny crystal heart quietly whispered,

"Anything,

anything,

ANYTHING'S POSSIBLE."

The sun set. Snow was beginning to fall softly, icing the emerald green window panes. There was a soft crunch, crunch under each passing booted foot.

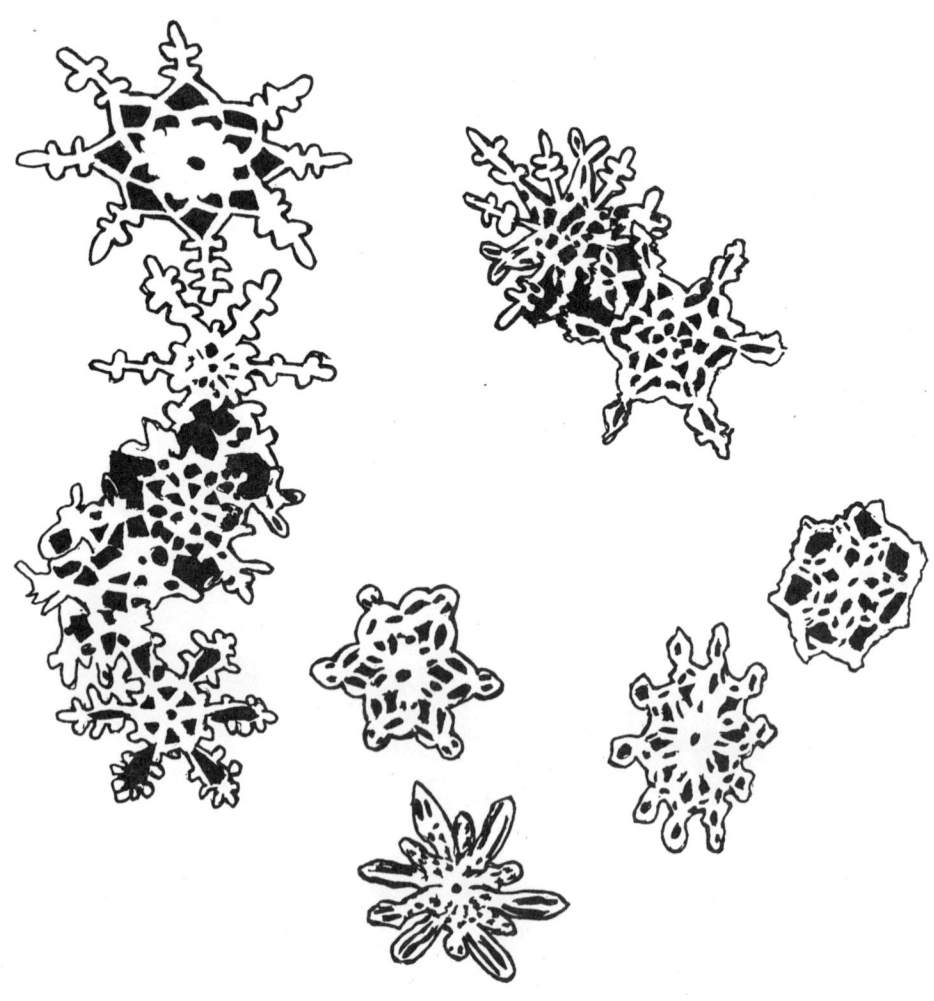

"Anything's possible," the tiny crystal heart quietly whispered.

"Anything,

anything,

ANYTHING'S POSSIBLE."

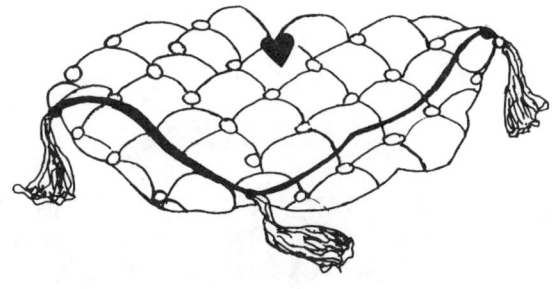

Stephanie Mellen

*T*he next morning the sad,
bent, crippled, balding
Shop Keeper wearing his
worn brown coat, scarf, hat,
and gloves put a large, shiny brass
key into the lock of the bright blue door,
turned the door knob, and slowly went inside,
closed the door, and

cried,

and cried,

and cried.

"Ooooh! Ah! How beautiful! I've never seen anything like that before!" sounded the words over and over again through the snow-iced emerald green window panes.

Slowly, the door knob turned on the bright blue shop door. Two sets of tiny booted footsteps could be heard.

"I'm closed - **F O R E V E R**!" said the Shop Keeper angrily to the small boy in the blue coat with the matching blue mittens.

"But why? How much are these?" the small boy asked in amazement, waving his blue-mittened hands toward the shop window, then pointing to the shelves and the floor.

The old Shop Keeper put his gnarled hand into his worn brown pants pocket. Slowly he pulled out a crumpled handkerchief. He wiped his tears. He blinked.

There in the shop window, on **every** shelf, on the floor were

hundreds and hundreds of cuddly soft crystal white stuffed rabbits of all shapes and sizes. Each one with a deep purple velvet bow trimmed with gold braid at the neck. Nestled in the center of each bow was a tiny iridescent crystal heart.

Stephanie Mellen

Day after day, week after week, month after month, each shattered iridescent crystal piece was transformed into one cuddly soft crystal white stuffed rabbit after another. Each one with a deep purple velvet bow trimmed with gold braid at its neck. Nestled in the center of each bow was a

tiny

iridescent

crystal heart.

One cuddly soft crystal white stuffed rabbit after another was held, loved, purchased, wrapped with a great deal of care in lavender paper covered with tiny crystal hearts by the gnarled hands of the old Shop Keeper and, taken home to *each* special child throughout the land and beyond.

"Anything,

anything,

ANYTHING IS POSSIBLE!"

quietly whispered the tiny iridescent crystal heart nestled in the center of the deep purple velvet pillow with gold tassels at each corner.

"ANYTHING'S POSSIBLE!"